CU00822689

FIFTEEN MYSTERIES IN THE LIFE OF JESUS

Visit our web site at
WWW.ALBAHOUSE.ORG

or call 1-800-343-2522 (ALBA)
and request current catalog

Fifteen Mysteries in the Life of Jesus

Reflections by Richard Hobbs

Preface by Raniero Cantalamessa, OFM Cap

ST PAULS

Alba
House

Library of Congress Cataloging-in-Publication Data

Hobbs, Richard (1933-1993).
   Fifteen mysteries in the life of Jesus : reflections / by Richard
Hobbs; preface by Raniero Cantalamessa.
      p. cm.
   ISBN:0-8189-0901-3 (alk. paper)
   1. Mysteries of the Rosary.   I. Title.

   BT303.H577 2001
   232.9—dc21

                                                    2001041301

Cover: Giovanni Bellini. *Madonna and Child* © Erich Lessing / Art
Resource, NY

Produced and designed in the United States of America by the
Fathers and Brothers of the Society of St. Paul,
2187 Victory Boulevard, Staten Island, New York 10314-6603,
as part of their communications apostolate.

ISBN: 0-8189-0901-3
ISBN: -085439-633-0

© Copyright 1998 E.K. Hobbs
© Copyright 2002 by the Society of St. Paul

Printing Information:

Current Printing - first digit   1   2   3   4   5   6   7   8   9   10

Year of Current Printing - first year shown

2002   2003   2004   2005   2006   2007   2008   2009   2010

Table of Contents

The Glorious Mysteries

Preface

In the early 1990's I would periodically receive from England short pieces written by Richard Hobbs. They were prophetic words — the kind one sometimes hears spoken aloud at charismatic prayer meetings. They nearly always focused on unity between Christians, concern for the poor, humility, and poverty of spirit. All of them contained rare insights and from the effect they had on those who heard them it was clear that these words were truly inspired.

I only had the chance of meeting Richard once, before the Lord called him to himself at the age of fifty-nine in 1993. The imposing presence of this typical English gentleman made his humility of spirit and childlike zeal all the more striking. It had not always been so. He had been educated at Eton, and was a successful businessman and father of six sons; he had held positions of responsibility and felt comfortable in a world of aristocracy and privilege, when "the Spirit of the Lord came upon him in power, and he prophesied with them and he was changed into a different person" (1 Samuel 10:6, MV).

He had become a Catholic at university but it was his later contact with the Charismatic Renewal that profoundly changed his life, and his prophetic gift was recognized by all. His words were measured, and were the fruit of long periods of prayer. He was very conscious of the responsibility of speaking words 'in the name of the Lord.' He was particularly concerned about how to resolve the problems of 'riches and poverty' and when praying about this subject he felt in his heart the same compassion and zeal which was revealed by the Christ of the Gospels.

After his death, his wife Elise, at the request of discerning friends, started publishing some of the writings which her husband had himself hoped to publish one day: a booklet entitled *the desire of My heart* (words expressing Jesus' desire for unity among all His followers); also a beautiful Via Crucis called *A More Perfect Way*, which has been suggested as a possible text to be used by the Pope for the Stations of the Cross in the Colosseum on Good Friday.

And now we have these moving reflections on

the Rosary. Here the emphasis is on the privilege of following the Cross, and of caring for the poor and the rejected. Also there is clearly a deep love for the Virgin Mary. Reading Richard's reflections on these mysteries in the life of Jesus one begins to understand how the Rosary can be a truly biblical prayer and a simple and direct way of penetrating into the heart of Christ and of the Gospel.

Raniero Cantalamessa, OFM Cap

Introduction

I remember that when I became a Roman Catholic in 1956, I carried a rosary in my pocket as a sort of badge of belonging. It had a comfortable feel, and it reminded me of the change that had taken place in my life, but I never used it. I had no idea how to say the rosary, not least because whenever I had heard it said in church, I couldn't actually make out what was being said. There seemed to be a meaningless dialogue between one person and the rest of the group which overlapped at times and was apparently in a foreign language. The noise continued for about 10 to 15 minutes and then most people got up and left the church. Sometimes I would hold my rosary in my hands during Mass because this seemed to be the thing to do, but those who did so never seemed to say anything. It was strange and very Catholic but not much of a help in my own spiritual life.

Then the Second Vatican Council opened up much warmer relationships with other churches and it seemed to me to be divisive and unnecessary to parade badges of difference like the rosary, which was not only repetitive prayer but also *appeared* to concentrate on Mary. I still carried a rosary, and sometimes tried to say it, now that I knew the prayers, but usually more as a penance than as an aid to devotion.

Distractions buzzed around inside my head as I tried desperately to concentrate on the third sorrowful mystery, feeling more and more guilty as the problems of tomorrow's management meeting replaced pious thoughts about the Crowning with Thorns. In some ways I was lucky, because I had been taken through the Bible as a child and so I had a fairly good grounding in Scripture which provided food for meditation whenever the distractions eased off for a second or so; but saying the rosary was not leading me deeper into the mystery of Jesus; it was simply a way of being religious, and keeping myself in a satisfactorily guilty frame of mind at my own inability to do it well.

In 1983 I discovered that God speaks to us through Scripture; some describe it as the words suddenly rising from the page and entering deep into the soul. Passages that I had read for years suddenly made sense and became alive in a way that affected my way of life. And the way that I made it possible for God to speak to me in this way through Scripture, the way in which I could become quiet enough to hear what He was saying, or still enough to listen, was by praying the rosary. I discovered that the rosary wasn't about Mary — she would have hated us to concentrate on her — but about her Son. Throughout each of the fifteen mysteries of the traditional cycles of the rosary, Mary points to Jesus, as she did throughout her life, saying again and again, "Do whatever He tells you." And as the years went by, I found that Jesus Himself seemed to be speaking to me, telling me about His mother or about the inner meaning of each of the events of His life that are contained in the rosary.

"The Word of God is something alive and active; it cuts more incisively than any two-edged sword: it can seek out the place where soul is divided from spirit, or joints from marrow; it can pass judgment on secret emotions and thoughts. No created thing is hidden from Him; everything is uncovered and stretched fully open to the eyes of the one to whom we must give an account of ourselves" (Hebrews 4:12-13). And the rosary, repetitive and apparently divisive, has been the window through which the two-edged sword of the Word of God has been able to gain access to my soul. Because it is repetitive it brings me back gently and firmly to the matter in hand; because it involves Mary, it concentrates on her Son as a real man whom I can know and with whom I can form a real relationship. And the rosary can do this because it involves the whole family of God, Father, Son and Holy Spirit, in their relationship with the daughter of God the Father, spouse of God the Holy Spirit, and mother of God the Son. It is as if we were brought directly into the family conversation, involved as participants and not just as an audience, asked to take part in the very life of the Trinity.

In fact it is only by involving Mary in our prayers in this way that we can make sure that we are not becoming too spiritual, too religious, but are keeping our feet on the ground. Jesus became a real human being in Mary's womb; He didn't spin Himself a body in heaven and then come down to earth; He took flesh in the same way that each one of us takes flesh, in our mother's body, and He could feel everything that we feel, suffer everything that we suffer. He got dirty, cut Himself, felt tired just as we do, and if we forget this, as we try to make Him suitably Godlike, then we have failed to understand the whole point of the Incarnation. Every time that we make Jesus sweet and clean and unruffled, we separate Him from the earth and we make Him unreal, a person who makes the sensitive feel guilty that they are not like Him, and the insensitive unashamed to carry on with their sinful lives. But He came to set us free and to call us to repentance, and He can only do those things if He is allowed to walk beside us where we are, sharing every part of our lives.

The rosary is a certain way of keeping our feet on the ground. It starts with the angel Gabriel asking a young unmarried girl to become the mother of God, progresses through the unjust trial and condemnation of that Son, and his death by the most cruel and barbaric method used by the Roman Empire, and ends with His call to His mother to come to be with Him in heaven. Every section can be illuminated by Scripture, seen through the eyes of Jesus, as if He spoke personally to us. I have tried to write down what I heard at each stage in the hope that this will encourage others to listen. The words are not intended to be recited, but to be pondered as Mary pondered on all the things that happened to her. If only everyone listened to God speaking to them; He is always doing so; it is just that we are not always listening. "Lord, to whom shall we go? You have words of eternal life. We believe and know that you are the Holy One of God" (John 6:68-69).

Richard Hobbs
Nov. 29, 1933 - Mar. 30, 1993

The Joyful Mysteries

Fra Angelico, *The Annunciation*. © Erich Lessing / Art Resource, NY

The Angel Gabriel asks Mary
to become the Mother of God

I did not come in power
to claim my kingdom.
I asked a humble, unmarried girl
if I could come,
flesh of her flesh,
as a child in her womb.
And not as a fully formed child
but as an embryo,
the smallest unit of humanity,
absolutely vulnerable
and dependent on my mother's care
both for herself and for me.

Can you imagine
the Creator of everything
contained within a single cell

of his own creature's body?
I did not seek special privileges;
I endured everything
that each one of you endures:
I risked my existence
just as each one of you risks
life and wholeness
in the months before you are born.

And if I entered my world
so courteously and quietly,
am I likely to enter your hearts
roughly and noisily?
Why are you afraid
to ask me in?
Have I not said
that those who ask
will be answered,
those who seek
will find?

I arranged everything
after my mother agreed
to accept me in her womb,
so that she would suffer
no humiliation.
When she consented

to be my mother,
she could have expected
to be repudiated by Joseph
and shamed publicly.
But I do not behave in that way;
I changed Joseph's perception
so that he gave my mother a home;
and I was subject to them both
for thirty years.

Why are you afraid
that if you let me into your hearts,
I will make you a mockery
among your family and friends,
an embarrassment among men?
Or that I will take over your lives
against your wills?
I come to set you free.

I did not send my angel Gabriel
to trick Mary or to enslave her,
but humbly to ask her
if she would be my mother.
I sent Gabriel because,
frightening though he was,
his appearance was nothing
compared to my uncovered glory.

And I had no covering for my glory
until my mother had consented
to clothe me with her flesh.

Open your hearts as she did,
and I will take on flesh again
in each one of you,
until the whole world
is full of my witnesses
and so is ready to receive me
as I come from my Father's right hand
on the clouds of heaven.

Mary goes immediately to help her cousin Elizabeth

My mother remained humble and simple,
even though she was the bride of the Holy Spirit
and the mother of God.
She did not set her eyes on lofty ambitions,
nor expect anyone to pay her homage as the
mother of a King.
She was content to remain a carpenter's wife,
and to set out immediately as a mother's help
to her cousin Elizabeth.

This is how peace will come on earth,
when all men and women do
the small things well
that they have to do every day;
and all seek to help their neighbors
when they need assistance.

When all keep their souls tranquil and quiet,
like children in their mothers' arms,
and praise God
because he has filled the hungry with good things
and exalted the lowly;
then my kingdom will have come on earth.

And this is the sign
that peace will come to the world,
that the meek will inherit the earth;
a baby in the womb recognizes me,
even though I am only just conceived,
and rejoices at the coming
of his Lord and Savior.
He did not come to me,
as the shepherds and the wise men
would come after my birth,
but I came to him
in the very first days
of my life on earth.
What a sign for your times,
my brothers and sisters.

How can you say
that your unborn children
are not individuals,
and that they have

no right to their own lives
if it is not convenient for you?
John knew me before my form
could be recognized as that of a man,
and his mother felt his greeting to me
and because of it believed
that my mother carried
her Lord and Savior within her.
Humble yourselves,
my brothers and sisters,
and realize
that you do not understand everything.
Turn to me and rejoice
that I have come among you again
in every child that is conceived.

For I am your elder brother,
but not at all like the one
of whose anger I spoke
in the story of the lost son:
because I watch, with my Father,
for the first sign of your return.
And we both run out to meet you,
and I, your brother, reach you first
so that I can carry you to your Father's arms
as he waits to receive you.
There is no jealousy in my heart at your coming,

for the earth is full of the good gifts of God
and there is more than enough for everyone.

And when you have received
the gifts prepared for you,
allow me to set out within you
— as I did when my mother heard
of her cousin's child —
for I can only run to meet my brothers in you.
So go with haste to meet
your brothers and sisters in their need
and help them from your fullness,
praising God for all his blessings
as you work with them
to bring me to birth once more in the world.

Jesus is born into the world

I was born,
a tiny baby,
in a stable
attached to an inn
in a village
in a small province
of a great empire.
I was a single flame in the darkness,
but not all the forces of darkness
since that time
have been able to put out the light
that I brought into the world.

And just as a flicker of light
brings joy and peace to the traveller
who is lost in the darkness,
so my light brings peace

to those who are near despair and hopeless,
oppressed by the world
and stifled by its cares and distractions.
Each heart is a stable
in which I can be born again;
and where I am,
there is light and life,
joy and peace.

I am waiting for you
to come to be counted
among my Father's children,
and then I can enter
the stable of your hearts
and fill you with my life.

Joseph and Mary travelled
to the town of David their ancestor,
to be registered,
and, in the same way,
you must turn your steps
towards your Father's house
to be numbered among his family.
Were not my first words,
"Why were you looking for me?
Did you not know
that I must be in my Father's house?"

And did I not start my ministry by saying,
"Turn back,
for the kingdom of heaven is close at hand"?

So I say again to you:
"Repent;
turn your faces
towards your Father's house;
come and be counted
among my brothers and sisters."
Then in the darkness
I will suddenly be born again within your hearts
and you will hear the angels singing,
"Glory to God in the highest heavens,
and peace on earth to men of good will."

But this is a promise,
a glimpse of the kingdom to come.
It is still dark
and you must take me into the world
as Joseph carried me into Egypt.
My birth within you is not the end
but the beginning of your journey.
You were in darkness
and now you have the light shining within you,
the life that is the light of men,
and the darkness

can neither understand
nor overpower my light.

Before you allow me
to be born within you,
you are lost.
But if you receive me,
you can see,
and I send you out into the darkness
to give light to those
who still live without my light.
For I must be born again
in all my brothers and sisters
until my light is over all
and there is no darkness left in the world.

Mary and Joseph redeem Jesus for two pigeons

The words of Simeon and Anna,
spoken about a young child
brought to the Temple
to be redeemed for two young pigeons
— the offering of poor people —
will be remembered forever.
The words of the priests,
rich people, and those in authority,
which were spoken at the same time,
are forgotten and will never be recalled.

I surface suddenly in the lives
of humble, powerless people.
But I will not enter those of the rich or powerful,
because they will try to arrest me
so that they can use me for their own purposes.

The joy of knowing that I am with them
remains in the hearts of the poor,
and the rich can never take away
that treasure from them.

But the rich are eaten up
by their frustration
that I cannot be bought,
or tamed,
or imprisoned
to make their lives more comfortable,
or to give them status and security.
I can be redeemed for two young pigeons;
I can be bought by a widow's mite;
I can be captured or imprisoned by love.
But your rich offerings out of your plenty,
your pious behavior
because you want to be seen as good,
your patronizing charity
to demonstrate your status,
these appall and repel me.

I am happy to laugh
with prostitutes and sinners
because they know that they need forgiveness.
And because they are despised

by those who think themselves to be good,
they know that they can get no help
from anyone but me.
But I was never at home at those gatherings
where my host judged my behavior
and barely tolerated my appearance,
and where I was given a role to play
that did not challenge
the self-importance of my fellow guests.

I am a light
to lighten those who will listen to me
and to be the glory of my people
— those who will follow me.
The humble and the poor are grateful
for the light offered by a little child,
and will follow
wherever I lead them.
And my light will illuminate their path
and help them to avoid
the dangers on the way.
But to the rich and powerful
my light will be an exposure
of their anger and pride,
because they look for a more suitable guide
and a light more fitting to their status.

I tell you again,
"Blessed are the poor
for theirs is the kingdom of heaven."

Jesus is lost and found again in the Temple

Where was the presence of God
when I sat among the teachers of the Law
in the Temple?
Was it in the Holy of Holies
within the Ark of the Covenant?
Or was it made flesh
and speaking with the teachers,
astounding them by the intelligence and wisdom
of the questions that they were asked?

I am the Word of God
made flesh and living among you.
My coming has changed forever
the way in which you are called.
The written law
and the remembered words of the prophets

only touch your minds:
but I have lived among you,
and you "have seen my glory,
the glory that I have from the Father
as the only Son of the Father,
full of grace and truth."
My presence among you
touches your hearts
if you believe in my name;
and so you are called in a new way.

You can search with your minds
and never find me,
but if you come to your Father's house
then I am there,
teaching the teachers
by listening and asking them questions.
And where is your Father's house?
It is within you.
Did I not say,
"If you love me,
you will keep my words,
and my Father will love you,
and we will come to you,
and make a home in you"?
We will do this

by sending the Holy Spirit into your hearts;
he will listen
to your inner thoughts and feelings,
and by asking questions
he will direct you on the right path,
the way that leads to everlasting life.

I must hide myself
so that you will search for me.
I have promised
that those who seek will find.
You will cry out in your sorrow and darkness
because you think that you have lost
the one whom you love.
Your hearts will be torn open by your mourning
so that the Father and I can come in
with the Spirit of Love
and dwell within you.
Then you will become temples of the living God,
lights in the darkness of the world,
witnesses to the Good News.

Once more the Word becomes flesh
and lives among men,
and those who live in darkness
can see my light.

The Sorrowful Mysteries

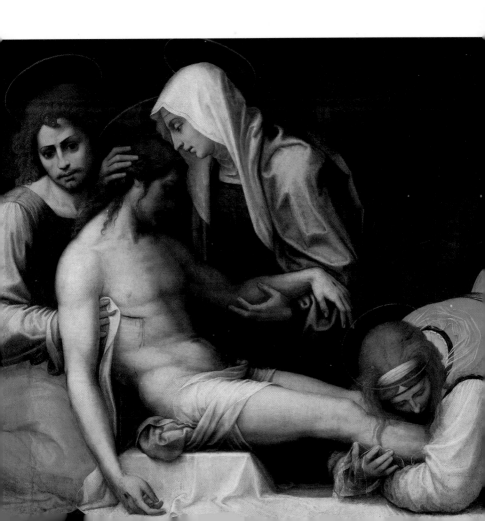

Fra Bartolomeo, *Deposition*. © Nimatallah / Art Resource, NY

Jesus is arrested in the Garden of Gethsemane

My Father would not set any bounds to his love,
and so I would not set any bounds to mine.
I had counted the cost of that decision,
and accepted it willingly
for love of you, my brothers and sisters.

I knew that I was to be arrested on that very night.
I knew who would lead the guards to me
at a time when they could expect
to find me asleep
and so unable to offer any resistance.
I knew what would follow my arrest,
and I experienced in my imagination
all the agonies that I would suffer the next day.

If I had not gone to the garden of Gethsemane,

but just a few fields further on,
Judas would not have found me
and he would have been punished
for misleading the Chief Priest and the Sanhedrin.
If I had told just a few of my friends
exactly what was going to happen,
they would have stayed awake
and guarded me through the whole night.
But I had been sent by my Father
to fulfill every last word of the Scriptures.

Still, I hoped
that like Isaac,
I should be saved at the last moment,
that my faith and trust
in my Father's love
would be enough.
And if there had been any other way,
then I knew that my Father would take it.

But as soon as I asked the question,
and in my heart I felt my Father weeping,
I knew that there was no other way.
Every word that he had put
into the lips of the prophets,
had to be seen to be fulfilled.

Nothing that comes from the lips of God
can be wasted;
nothing is ever spoken unnecessarily.

My Father could only send
an angel to comfort me.
Everything was now in my hands;
the fate of creation rested on my decision.
In the beginning,
I had created everything
at my Father's command
and now it was for me to agree
to recreate everything
as my Father had wanted it to be.

My brothers and sisters,
can you imagine my agony
as I struggled to stay in that garden,
knowing the horrors that lay ahead?

None of you will ever have to suffer
as I did in the garden,
because I was the first among you to do so,
and you have my example to give you hope.
You know, as I did not,
that your death to yourself

will not leave you dead but empty
so that I can pour new life into you.

For me, the garden was all darkness,
leading to even greater darkness.
I could see and accept
the sacrifice that was necessary,
but I could not see the reward that followed.
Whenever you find yourself in the garden
remember that I am there with you,
and rejoice that I will lead you
from there into new life.

Jesus is scourged by the soldiers

You saw my glory,
the glory of my faithful love.
You could not bear my uncovered glory,
the blazing Sun of Righteousness
that will shine on earth in the last days.
I showed you my glory in a different way,
the way of sacrifice,
of willing offering for your sins
and for the sins of the whole world;
in this way
the power of Satan would be broken forever
and you would be free
to walk once more with your God
in the evening of the world.

Only those who know
the cost of self-offering

will see my glory.
Those who strive for honor,
for worldly success and the praises of men,
even though they do these things
for entirely honest reasons,
will never see my glory.
The bleeding wounds from the scourging,
the crown of thorns and the purple robe,
the nails and the naked man
stretched out on the cross,
these are the signs of my glory,
veiled so that you can bear it,
and then by imitating me,
come to know from your own experience
the depths of my love for you.

The cruelty of my scourging
was the work of men
who did not know me
as an individual.
To them I was an unknown criminal,
a Jew,
a religious maniac,
a prisoner.

How many times
have you done the same

to the stranger in your midst?
Each man and woman
is your brother or your sister,
to be cherished and embraced,
treated as a member of your family,
listened to and cared for
as an individual with a name.
Look into the eyes
of those you meet
and offer them yourselves.
Those who scourged me
would not look into my eyes.

I did not condemn them.
How could they understand
what they were doing?
Even my own people
could not understand
that their God,
the God of Sinai,
had come to earth
and become a man like them
to share their human existence.
My life was a blasphemy
to those who believed
in a God of laws and power,
who would punish the sinful

and reward the law-abiding.
How could they understand
that the glory of their God
is love and not power,
and that the greatest possible love
is to lay down life for a friend?

The kingdom
that I came to proclaim
is a kingdom of love.
Not all those
who call themselves Christians
are citizens of that kingdom.
Only those who look into their brothers' eyes,
or who embrace their sisters,
and truly offer themselves
as living sacrifices for their friends,
are members of my body.

Those who judge and condemn
and punish in my name,
still scourge me
and shut themselves off
from my healing love.
Look into my eyes
and I will heal you,
my beloved people.

Jesus is crowned with thorns and shown to the people

Why did my Father give you power over me?
Because he wanted me to get very close to you
to show you the depths of his love for you;
not the distant love of a God
who sits on a throne in his heaven
and looks down on you on the earth,
but the love of a Father who longs to help you
to carry your burdens,
to comfort and heal you,
to give you every good gift.
He wants to come into your homes,
and to sit with you at your meals
as one of the family.
He wants to walk with you
as a beloved friend.
He could not do that himself

and so he sent me, his only Son,
to make his love known to you.

I could take on your weakness
and then act out my Father's name which is Love.
Can you truly imagine the love of God?
Can you understand the depth
of your Father's love for you?

The Father sent me to show you his love,
and to act it out among you
to give you an example to copy.
I am the image of your unseen Father;
in my life, and particularly in my passion,
I showed you the depths
to which love must be prepared to go.
There is no room for fear in love,
no room for shame,
no excuses,
no holidays.
Love offers everything
and expects no return.

You cannot bear the unveiled love of God.
It falls like a fire upon you
and you are consumed and burnt up in its heat.

You are not ready yet to be refined
and purified by the naked flame
of your Father's love for you,
and so it has to be filtered,
mediated to you through my flesh.

My crown of thorns is one of the ways
in which I show you the Father's love.
To you it appears
only as an agonizing, undeserved punishment,
but I accepted it without complaint
to show you the depths of my love,
and so of my Father's love for you.
For me the pain was nothing
in comparison to the ache in my heart for you,
my long lost brothers and sisters.

And look
at what has happened
to the crown of thorns
as a result of my acceptance.
It has become more valuable
than the finest gold,
so that kings would have given
every other jewel in their crowns
to be allowed to possess

even a single thorn from mine.
Just as my Father's love
makes and perfects everything,
so my love renews, restores and changes
what is an ugly instrument of punishment
into an object of honor and respect.

What are the intentions in your heart?
Is there nothing
but love for God and for your neighbor?
Or is there something left
of striving for your own comfort and position?
You cannot be free
until there is nothing of your own self left
in your heart.

If you try to save your own life,
you will lose it
and suffer torments in the process.
But if you willingly and obediently
offer up your own life,
you will find that it has been given back to you
increased ten thousand fold,
and that the giving up
has been far easier
than you could ever imagine.

If my thoughts had been
of my own comfort and life
when they pressed
the crown of thorns on my head,
the pain would have been unendurable.
But my thoughts were all of you,
my brothers and sisters,
and that made the agony bearable,
for I longed to complete my sacrifice
so that you would be able
to go out into the world
and tell everyone of my love.

Jesus carries His Cross through Jerusalem

I could only manage one step at a time;
I did not see the grand design at that moment.
I could only summon my strength
to take the next step,
to carry the crosspiece on my shoulders
until I could carry it alone no longer
and they made Simon help me.
I was obedient to those
who led me to Calvary,
and I did nothing to protest
against their injustice and cruelty.
Who recognized their Lord and their God in me?
What God would allow himself to be treated
in such a humiliating and agonizing way?

Do you not see?
Anyone can bow down

before a god of power and majesty;
the gods of all the peoples of the world
do god-like things,
either behaving with power to crush all opposition
and to reward their friends with goods and honors,
or behaving with great and obvious holiness,
fasting and praying without ceasing.
Satan himself behaves in a way
that many think is truly god-like.

But I allowed myself to be treated
like a common criminal,
despised and rejected by men,
and nailed to a cross to die.
And I ask you to follow my example
out of love for me.

Every other god
is a creation of your imaginations,
yourselves written large in fantasy,
bigger, better, holier than you are.
But I am not interested
in your following me
for what you can get
by putting yourselves under
my lordship and protection.
I want to know your hearts;

do you love me
in whatever disguise I appear to you?
And so I walk the world
in the poor, the rejected,
the sick and the oppressed.
Do you love me
and recognize me in them?

Would your heart have gone out to me
as I walked, step by step, to Calvary?
Would you have offered
to share the weight of my cross?
Would you have wiped my face with a cloth?
Would you have given me
a drink to soothe my pain?
Or would you have turned away
because I could not possibly be your God,
because a God worth following
could never allow himself
to be treated in such a way?

But I tell you,
if you do not recognize me
in those who still carry a cross,
then I will not recognize you
when I come again in glory.
You will know me then,

but so will everyone else;
my glory will be unmistakable.
But I will not recognize you
unless you recognized me
when my glory was hidden
in those who cried out for your love.

I am the perfect image of the Father
and our name is Love.
You cannot call us by that name
because you can only pronounce it effectively
by doing it.
Your lips can speak falsehood,
but your actions will always tell the truth.
It is useless to repeat the right words;
I am not deceived.

Do not weep for me,
but for your children
on whom the judgment
that follows from injustice
will be executed.
Go out and offer help
to those who are carrying
the cross of poverty,
of loneliness,

of false imprisonment.
Then you will find me
because where there is love,
you make me live once more among you.
Only in this way
can you turn aside the judgment
that you have called down on your children
by your pride and selfishness.

Take up your cross and follow me,
for only those who lose their lives for my sake
will find them.

Jesus is nailed to His Cross and dies

The lamb does not know its fate
and when it is slaughtered
it is killed quickly.
But I knew what lay ahead
when I surrendered myself in the garden,
and my death was slow,
and made deliberately painful
by those to whom I gave power over me.
Yet I did not complain
but asked my Father
to forgive those who wounded me
because they had no idea
what they were really doing.
I offered myself up to my Father
to take away the sins of the world.
Every sin ever committed in all of time
is redeemed by my sacrifice.

All nature knew what was being done;
only men were blind and deaf.

How can you call yourselves my disciples
if you hold anything back?
My Father sent me
to offer a perfect sacrifice to him
and I kept nothing.
I offered myself as the victim
on the altar of the Cross,
placed there by the accusations
of the chief priests of my own people,
their final sacrifice
— though they did not know it —
and the only one
that was completely effective
and did not need to be repeated.

I frustrate the evil intentions of men
and turn their wickedness into good.
For it was necessary
that I should be offered up
as the Lamb of God.
Yet if anyone had killed me
knowing that he was killing the Son of God,
how could he escape everlasting punishment?

It was only because they did not understand,
because their eyes were blind and their ears deaf,
that I could be offered up
by the leaders of my people
and yet they could be forgiven
even before repenting of their actions.

But there is no excuse for those
who crucify me today.
Every time you refuse
to feed the hungry,
to make strangers welcome,
to clothe the naked,
to visit the sick
or those in prison,
you fail to do these things to me.
And I look down from the Cross
— where you have nailed me
so that you can worship me with your rituals,
and where I am safe
because I cannot move among you
and touch your hearts —
and I see the pain
of those you have not helped.
They are my body
and if you do not suffer with them

and try to ease their pain and your own,
you cannot be part of my body.
For the whole body suffers
when any part is in pain.

Take me down
from the place
where you have nailed me
with your religion,
and let me walk freely among you
and heal you.
For I am a living God
and you are my people.

The Glorious Mysteries

Giovanni Bellini, *The Pesaro Altarpiece.* © Alinari / Art Resource, NY

Jesus rises from the dead in New Life

It is not enough
to be born in the flesh;
each one of you
must be born again from above
as I was.
I invite each one of you
to follow me, and to come to my Father's table.
But my way goes through death to self,
through the crucifixion of everything
you have received in your first birth.
Everything must be transformed
by being surrendered to me,
so that you can receive it back from me.

You had no choice in your first birth;
I give you choice in your second.

Everything surrendered
and then accepted back from my hands,
is clearly gift and not your own.
That is the meaning of my resurrection;
I have shown you the way
by giving my Spirit
into my Father's hands,
and then accepting it back
on the morning of my resurrection.

You cannot have peace in your hearts
until you have been born again from above.
And you cannot understand the meaning of peace
until you have surrendered your whole lives to me
and received them back as pure gift.
You may refuse my invitation
to sit at my Father's table,
and your worldly lives
may seem to be filled with meaning,
to be more real than the lives
of those who walk with me.
But until you have experienced
the peace that comes
from my Spirit within you,
you do not know
the meaning of true peace.

Because all that you have in the flesh,
all the good things
that you store up for yourselves,
everything can be taken away from you,
leaving you poor and broken.
And so if you live in worldly comfort,
you can never know peace;
you have to defend your riches,
and exclude others from your way of life.
Possessions become a burden,
and position an endless worry
in case someone stronger takes it from you.

But those who have surrendered
everything into my hands,
will receive back all that they need;
they walk with me
in the freedom of my resurrection life;
they ask and it is given to them;
they knock and I open to them;
if they are weary,
I take their burdens from them;
nothing disturbs their peace,
even though they walk
through the valley of the shadow of death.

My resurrection is a sign of freedom,
freedom from all worries and from fear.
I surrendered my Spirit to my Father,
and received back new life,
life that death can never touch again.
My death was my final word to you;
if you understand it and do it,
then you will be free.
When you receive every moment as gift,
and keep back nothing for yourself,
then you will know true peace,
the peace that the world cannot give,
the peace that only those
who have been born again from above,
can ever know.

Jesus goes up to Heaven to His Father's right hand

Was I unhappy to go back
to the glory of heaven,
leaving my disciples leaderless?
Was there a flurry
of last minute instructions?
No,
it was a time of peace
and without sadness,
because I knew that the Holy Spirit
would supply all the knowledge
that my disciples needed
and that in the Holy Spirit
they would be one with me
at all times.
But to many
it seemed an odd and inconclusive

end to my life on earth.
After the excitement of the Resurrection
I was just lifted up
out of the sight of my disciples.
But I had disappeared before
so how did they know
that this was the last time
that they would walk with me on earth?

It was the best way
to hand over responsibility to them.
If I had made it a solemn occasion,
they would have been crushed
by the sorrow of parting
and by the responsibility
that was laid upon them
without me to guide them.
But as it was,
they went back to Jerusalem like children,
rejoicing over the promise
that I would send the Spirit,
ready to continue that life of prayer together
that I had joined on several occasions
after my Resurrection.

They were not in mourning
because they would see me no more,

closed in on themselves in their grief;
they were full of the joy
of their renewed fellowship with me,
and looking forward
to what I had promised,
that I would send my Holy Spirit upon them
and that I myself would be with them always.
I had washed them in water
before my passion,
and so now they were ready
to accept their baptism of fire,
of the Holy Spirit.

They were to be my witnesses;
on them I had placed the responsibility
for preaching the Good News
to the whole world.
If I had not gone back to my Father,
which one of them would have left Jerusalem
to go to the nations?
Would they not all
have stayed near me?

But before I went back,
in the same way that I will come again,
they worshipped me.
And they finally understood

what Peter and James and John had seen
on the mountain of the Transfiguration.
And having understood the glory that is to come,
they went back to Jerusalem
still dazzled by what they had seen,
and determined to do all that they could
to hasten the day
when I come again.

And generation by generation
their vision has been handed down
so that it has fallen to you,
my brothers and sisters,
to work to bring it to pass
in your day.
I have gone up
so that I may be ready to come down.
I am not delaying my return,
but I will only come
when you have completed the work
that I have given you.
I long to say once more to my Father,
"It is finished",
but I cannot
until those words are truth,
because I am the Truth.

I am in your hands;
I have handed over the whole task
of bringing creation to completion to you.
I have given you all the tools you need
through the Holy Spirit.
and now I can only wait
and make everything ready
for my return.

Reap the fields that I have sown
and gather the harvest into my barns.

The coming of the Holy Spirit in the Upper Room

My Spirit will only enter where he is welcomed;
he will only give the gifts of knowledge and power
where he can give them freely
and unconditionally;
he will only remain where he is in control.
For the Spirit everything is possible,
and so he will only act
when it is in accordance with the Father's will.
His power cannot be under your control;
such power cannot be exercised by creatures.
Do you wonder
that my Spirit does not flow freely
among the rich people of the world?
They try to control everything,
and to use everything safely
so that they never risk becoming poor.

At Pentecost
those filled with the Spirit
appeared to be drunk,
yet they were filled with power
and spoke of the marvelous works of God
in all the languages of those who heard them.
The Spirit must fill every part of you
and take control of everything you do.
You must do nothing to control
what the Spirit does.
It may seem to be foolish,
but only in the eyes of the worldly.
You must yield yourself
to the Love that is the Spirit
and be carried wherever he wills,
for Love will never lead you to any harm.

Do not be ashamed
of what the Spirit does.
Just allow yourself
to be filled by him
and carried wherever he wills,
just as those in the Upper Room
were filled and used
at the first Pentecost.

I will pour out my Spirit
on all men and women,
and those who accept will be filled
with the power of the Love of God.
This is the community
that I am calling together
in these days,
the community of those
who have received the Spirit
willingly and with joy.

These are my beloved brothers and sisters,
the family of my Father,
the kingdom come on earth.
They do not lord it over those
who do not accept the Spirit,
but go out in love to them,
and try to bring them
to understanding and repentance.
They will not break the crushed reed
nor snuff out the faltering wick.
They have no thought for their own comfort,
but go out
to open the eyes of the blind,
to free captives
from the prison of their unbelief,

and those who live in darkness
from the dungeon of their ignorance.

The Spirit still hovers
over the troubled waters of the world,
and will do so
until all is made new,
and the kingdom has come
on earth as it is in heaven.

Mary is taken up
body and soul into Heaven

A child's dreams are real;
a child believes what is said
and believes it to be literally true;
woe to those who abuse the trust of a child.

Mary, my mother, remained childlike
throughout her life;
she believed the message of the angel,
and the words of Simeon and Anna;
above all she believed my words,
even when it seemed
that I had failed,
and that my words were false.
She accepted everything into her heart
and pondered on it,
until it made sense.

Ten thousand years
would not have been enough
for her to exhaust
all that she could ponder,
for there is no limit to me,
and no one can answer
every question about me.
Even so, my mother would have been content
to ponder on my words and actions,
gradually teasing out
their full meaning.

But what would you have done to her
if I had left her among you?
You would have made her
into an idol, a goddess;
you would have fought to own her
to give your party
power over your brothers and sisters;
you would have used her words,
or her silences,
to prove your own point of view;
and you would have forgotten me.
She would have ceased to be
the mother of your unity,
and she would have become

a curiosity and a scandal,
the source of divisions among you.

And so I cut short her pondering
and brought her into the place
where every question is answered.
I needed no more proof of her love,
nor of her faithfulness.
So why should she remain among you?
A mother must allow her children
to become separate from her
and to make their own decisions;
and all heaven longed for her company.
And so I called her to me,
and she came like a little child.
She believed in her dream
and woke up to find it was true.

She lives for ever
in my company in heaven.

Mary is crowned Queen of Heaven and the whole company of Heaven rejoices

How can a creature be Queen of Heaven?
What kind of kingdom is it
in which the widow of a carpenter
is raised to the highest rank
and the whole company of saints rejoices?
How can a creature be royal
in the presence of God?

Did I not say
that you were a chosen race,
a royal priesthood,
a people set apart?
I have called you out of darkness
and into my wonderful light.
I have destined you all for thrones in heaven,

for you are all made to be saints.
And none of this could happen
unless Mary agreed to become the mother of God.
The gates of heaven could not open
to allow you in,
for though you were made in the image of God,
you made that image unrecognizable through sin.
Only through the perfect image of the Father,
the beloved Son,
could the gates of heaven
be opened again to man.

And the kingdom that you enter
through the gates that I have opened
is like an endless wedding feast.
My mother is there in the midst of it
but the wine of joy never runs out
because I supply all that is needed,
and more than enough.
And so there is no need for her to tell me
when it is running short.

The company of the saints,
— the attendants on the Bridegroom —
surround my mother,
and their oil of gladness never runs dry
because they have stored up

treasure for themselves in heaven
while they lived their lives on earth.
They were always ready for my coming,
and rejoiced to hear my voice.
Their lights will never go out
and their joy will never end.
But their waiting seemed like death
to many of their companions on earth.
They did not think of their own success or status;
they did not store up riches and possessions
to ensure their own worldly comfort.

They encouraged one another
when I seemed to be far away,
by remembering my words
and what I had done to call them to my service.
And when they heard my voice calling them,
they never hesitated to enter
by the ladder that leads to the gates of heaven.

What is the ladder
that leads from earth to heaven
by which all men and women
may be lifted up into my presence?
It is the Cross.
It is the only way
by which you can come

to the wedding feast.
All other ways
of your own building
are like the tower of Babel —
they lead to quarrels and disunity.

But the Cross unites all those
who accept it
and climb by it into my presence.
For they have done
whatever I told them,
and so for them
I will turn water into wine,
tears into joy,
pain and suffering into wedding garments.

Heaven is only heaven
for those who have not tried
to keep their lives
and to make them
as comfortable as possible.
If YOU are in the center of your life,
then the wedding feast of heaven
will be hell for you.
All eyes there are on the Bridegroom,
on me as your King,
and on Mary,

whom I have crowned Queen,
and on my Bride —
the company of the saints,
my Church,
my own Body.

My saints do not worry about themselves
at that banquet,
about where they are sitting,
or how they are dressed,
or what they have to feast on.
All eyes are on me,
the Lamb who was slain,
and on the consummation of my love for you.
At that table
you will understand at last
the everlasting mystery of your God,
the endless play of love
between the Father and me,
the Love that is
the Holy Spirit.

You will be part of that Love,
both object and source at the same time.
For you will be at that table
through me, and in me and with me.
And you will forget yourselves

and everything that you have been
in the glory
of the fulfillment of all things,
the end for which everything was created,
to be loved by God
and to love God
for ever and ever,
Amen.

The Glory of the Lord

You are made to be
like bright stars
shining in the night,
glittering pinpricks of light,
making the darkness bearable
for lonely travelers
far from home.

When every shining piece
is in its place in the heavens,
then there will be no night,
nothing but a vault
that reflects my glory,
and in my brightness
nothing can be hidden.

ST PAULS

This book was produced by St. Pauls/Alba House, the
Society of St. Paul, an international religious congregation of
priests and brothers dedicated to serving the Church through
the communications media.

For information regarding this and associated ministries of
the Pauline Family of Congregations, write to the Vocation
Director, Society of St. Paul, P.O. Box 189, 9531 Akron-
Canfield Road, Canfield, Ohio 44406-0189. Phone (330)
702-0396; or E-mail: spvocationoffice@aol.com or check our
internet site, www.albahouse.org